AF143912

BOOK ANALYSIS

Written by Hadrien Seret and Célia Ramain

Translated by Emma Hanna

The Hobbit

BY J. R. R. TOLKIEN

Some questions to think about...

J. R. R. TOLKIEN

ENGLISH WRITER

- **Born in Bloemfontein (South Africa) in 1892.**
- **Died in Bournemouth (United Kingdom) in 1973.**
- **Notable works:**
  - *The Hobbit* (1937), children's tale
  - *The Lord of the Rings* (1954-1956), fantasy trilogy
  - *The Silmarillion* (1977), anthology

J. R. R. Tolkien was an English writer and university professor. Although he is best-known for his *The Lord of the Rings* trilogy, he was in fact the creator of an entire fictional universe, which he used as the setting for poems (*The Adventures of Tom Bombadil*, 1962), fairy tales and legends (*Unfinished Tales of Númenor and Middle-Earth*, 1980). Fuelled by a tremendous love of language, literature and mythology, Tolkien's imagination spawned an entire universe populated with fantastic creatures, many of which are now considered staple archetypes of fantasy fiction.

This universe served as the setting for such meticulously detailed stories that Tolkien is often credited with both founding and giving credibility to the genre of modern fantasy.

THE HOBBIT

THE PREQUEL TO *THE LORD OF THE RINGS*

- **Genre:** fantasy novel
- **Reference edition:** Tolkien, J. R. R. (2011) *The Hobbit*. London: HarperCollins.
- **1ˢᵗ edition:** 1937
- **Themes:** magic, quests, war, betrayal, alliances

The Hobbit was J. R. R. Tolkien's first novel. It was published in 1937, and was awarded the *New York Herald Tribune*'s prize for best children's novel the following year.

The story follows the adventures of Bilbo, a hobbit whose peaceful life is thrown into chaos when the wizard Gandalf ropes him into taking part in a perilous quest. Along with 13 dwarves, he must overcome all kinds of setbacks and trials in order to reach the Lonely Mountain, where a priceless treasure hoard is jealously guarded by the dragon Smaug. Bilbo is only able to see the quest through and return home thanks to his own wits and the powers of a mysterious magic ring – the very same ring that the plot of *The Lord of the Rings* hinges on.

SUMMARY

THE DRAGON SMAUG

A few hundred years before Bilbo sets off on his adventures, the dragon Smaug lived in the Grey Mountains. One day, he learns of the treasures that the dwarves have hoarded in the Lonely Mountain. Driven by greed, he attacks the surrounding towns, killing many of the dwarves and forcing the survivors into exile. He then claims the Lonely Mountain as his own, and spends the next two hundred years there, watching over his precious hoard. However, he is eventually driven out and killed by a hobbit and a band of dwarves who are determined to reclaim their treasure.

AN UNEXPECTED JOURNEY

Bilbo Baggins is a middle-aged hobbit – 50 years old, to be precise – with a placid temperament. His parents were from two very different families: the Bagginses, who are exceptionally steady in nature and loathe surprises; and the Tooks, who have a very adventurous spirit. He leads a peaceful life until the day the wizard Gandalf, who is famous for his many astonishing feats, ropes him into going on an adventure, accompanied by 13 dwarves: Fili, Kili, Dwalin, Balin, Nori, Dori, Ori, Oin, Gloin, Bifur, Bofur, Bombur, and their leader, Thorin Oakenshield. This motley crew has a simple goal: to recover the priceless riches guarded by the dragon Smaug inside the Lonely Mountain – the rightful inheritance of Thorin Oakenshield. They believe that they will be able to achieve this goal because Thorin has a key which will grant them access to a secret passageway, as well as a mysterious map which will be deciphered by the elf Lord Elrond. However, the company still needs an experienced burglar to steal the hoard from under the monster's nose – a role which is filled by Bilbo, on Gandalf's advice, in spite of vocal opposition to this plan from the hobbit himself. As it turns out, Bilbo has the advantage of being able to move about without making a sound.

Now that the company has been assembled, they are able to set off on their adventure. Trouble soon befalls them along the way: lost in a forest and drawn to a mysterious light shining in the middle of the night, Bilbo and the dwarves are captured by three trolls who plan to roast them over their campfire and eat them. However, they are rescued by Gandalf, who tricks the trolls into squabbling among each other until the sun rises and turns them to stone. Following this, they are forced to take shelter in a cave when stone giants start tossing rocks at them, only to be kidnapped by goblins while they are sleeping and carried off to their underground lair. Only Gandalf is able to evade capture. The goblins bring the company before their king, who sentences the prisoners to death, but a spell cast by Gandalf causes sudden confusion, allowing Thorin and his friends to escape. However, during their flight, Bilbo trips and tumbles into a chasm.

GOLLUM AND HIS PRECIOUS RING

Lost in the labyrinthine tunnels of the goblins' lair, the hobbit stumbles upon a gold ring. Unaware of its true value, he pockets it. Soon afterwards, he meets Gollum, a sinister creature who offers to lead him out of the caves, but only if he wins at a game of riddles – and if Bilbo loses, he will be eaten. The hobbit wins, but Gollum refuses to keep his promise. As he advances towards Bilbo, preparing to eat him, Bilbo stumbles, and the ring happens to slip onto his finger, turning the hobbit invisible. Bilbo takes advantage of this new ability and follows Gollum to the surface, where he is reunited with the rest of the company – though he keeps his good fortune a secret from them.

Aided by wolves, the goblins continue pursuing the group, and eventually corner them on top of a rocky outcropping, where they are forced to climb into the trees to escape. They are saved by eagles at the very last moment, and taken to their eyries. Gandalf then takes them to Beorn, a hermit with the ability to transform into a bear. Beorn warns the dwarves about the dangers of Mirkwood forest, which they will have to pass through in order to reach the Lonely Mountain. When they reach the edge of the forest, Gandalf bids them farewell, saying that he has urgent business elsewhere. The company continues their journey in much lower spirits, and various mishaps immediately befall them – they are captured firstly by ravenous giant spiders, and then by the wood-elves, whose feasts were disrupted by the dwarves on several occasions. However, Thorin and his followers are eventually saved from their misfortune by Bilbo's ingenuity and the powers of his magic ring.

THE LONELY MOUNTAIN

Having overcome all of these obstacles, the group finally reaches the Lonely Mountain. Using their leader's map and key, the dwarves manage to enter the mountain through a hidden door. This allows them to avoid confronting Smaug directly, and Bilbo is sent ahead as a scout to determine whether or not the dragon is still alive. Using his magic ring, the hobbit manages to steal a tiny portion of the treasure, all while holding a conversation with Smaug, whose pride is so great that he even shows off his gemstone armour, which has a weak spot. After the burglar leaves, Smaug realises that he has been stolen from, and decides to take revenge on the inhabitants of Lake-town, whom he holds responsible. He is eventually defeated by the archer Bard, who has been informed of the monster's weak spot by a thrush.

The dwarves take advantage of the dragon's

departure to fortify the mountain, and marvel over the treasures hidden throughout the dragon's lair. However, Thorin cannot find the most precious treasure of all: the Arkenstone, a priceless stone which shines like a star. He has no idea that Bilbo has the stone, having picked it up and pocketed it, unaware of its value or its importance.

Bard decides to demand compensation from the dwarves in light of the destruction wreaked upon his town, and for his extraordinary feat of slaying the dragon. Although Bard is accompanied to the meeting by the elf-king himself, Thorin refuses his request point-blank. Bilbo then sneaks out of the mountain and gives Bard the Arkenstone, hoping that this will compel the dwarf to pay what is owed and break the stalemate. However, Thorin is unmoved, and banishes Bilbo for treason. He then sends a message to his cousin Dain, asking him to bring his army to help consolidate the dwarves' position. As the dispute between the three sides turns into an all-out battle, Gandalf appears and warns them that a contingent of goblins and wolves is preparing to launch a surprise attack against them. The dwarves, elves and humans are then forced to band together to repel the invaders in what later becomes known as the Battle of Five Armies. Thorin is killed during this battle, but not before expressing his remorse for his actions towards Bilbo. Having been paid handsomely for his services, the hobbit returns home, where he is finally able to enjoy a well-deserved rest.

CHARACTER STUDY

BILBO BAGGINS

Bilbo Baggins is the main character of *The Hobbit*. Although his father was a Baggins, a well-known family whose members "never had any adventures or did anything unexpected" (p. 3), his mother was a Took, and "once in a while members of the Took-clan would go and have adventures" (p. 4). Throughout the story, the hero is torn between these two opposing sides of his personality, with the dominant trait at any given moment largely depending on what kind of trouble he is dealing with. Until Gandalf leaves them on the edges of Mirkwood forest, it is his Baggins side that generally remains at the forefront. Roped into a quest that he had no desire to go on, Bilbo spends his time complaining about the hardships of the journey and dreaming of splendid breakfasts. He is not really invested in their quest, and his role in it seems distant and vague, so he simply endures the misfortunes that befall him (the trolls, being captured by the goblins, etc.) and, like the dwarves, relies on Gandalf to rescue him from danger.

Winning the game of riddles against Gollum and finding the magic ring are turning points for him, and allow him to gradually become aware of his own abilities and toughen up a bit, as shown by the growing respect that Thorin and his company have for him. As Bilbo's Took side comes to the fore, it enables him to step into the role of a helper that had previously been played by the wizard, meaning that he is able to chase off the giant spiders, and then save the dwarves from the elves' dungeons by planning their escape. Naming his sword "Sting" after going on his first solo adventure is a symbol of that change: when the hero takes his anonymous sword and gives it a name that has a ring of bravery, it reflects how he has cast off his fears to reveal "a different person, and much fiercer and bolder" (p. 144).

At the end of the story, Bilbo finally manages to find a balance between the two sides of his personality. The position he takes up during the Battle of Five Armies is a perfect illustration of his newly balanced outlook, as he finds himself in the only spot from which it is possible to retreat (symbolising his Baggins side), but which is also where they will make their last stand if they are defeated (symbolising his Took side). This new attitude spurs Gandalf to remark that the hobbit is no longer the same person he used to be – by the time he returns to the peaceful life that he was suddenly whisked away from at the start of the novel, he has matured immensely and become a much braver character.

THORIN OAKENSHIELD

Thorin is the direct descendant of the dwarf kings who ruled over the Lonely Mountain. As such, he should have ascended to the throne upon the death of his ancestors, but was unable to do so because of Smaug's attack. Despite living in exile for many years, he has no intention of surrendering his ancestors' kingdom and riches to the dragon, and believes that he will one day see his rightful inheritance restored to him. With this goal in mind, he organises the quest that Gandalf and Bilbo take part in. Thorin is very aware of his own importance, and proves to be an extremely proud, haughty dwarf, exuding a constant contempt which, more often than not, is directed at Bilbo. He never misses a chance to question his burglar's abilities or to act as though his presence is a burden. However, his jabs become much more infrequent after Bilbo saves the company, even if they never disappear completely (for example, he complains about their travelling conditions during their escape in the barrels, and neglects to thank the hobbit for freeing them). His sharp tongue and his enormous ego are complemented by a tendency to rely solely on his own cohort in order to achieve his goals, all while remaining comparatively passive compared to the efforts of Gandalf and Bilbo.

Ingratitude, greed and selfishness are other traits that can be added to this unflattering portrait, as he refuses to compensate Bard and the elf-king for their help in the fight against Smaug. He even sends his burglar away when he learns that Bilbo smuggled the Arkenstone into enemy hands, never comprehending that the situation is chiefly of his own making. However, the Battle of Five Armies gives him a chance to redeem himself when he leads a decisive assault against the goblins and the wolves. He is mortally wounded, and eventually expresses his remorse for his behaviour towards Bilbo just before he dies, sealing his legacy as a noble spirit, even though this was a side of his character that rarely shone through while he was alive.

GANDALF

When the story opens, Gandalf is described as an old man who is famous both for finding adventures everywhere he goes and for his marvellous fireworks. In fact, when the wizard visits Bilbo at the start of the story, the hobbit's clearest memories of him are of his fireworks. However, Gandalf is more than just a purveyor of fabulous fireworks. Firstly, the dwarves view his authority as absolute: he is the one who chooses Bilbo to be their burglar, provides them with the map and the key to the secret passageway to enter the Lonely Mountain, and advises the company about the decisions they should make and the routes they should follow. He is able to do so thanks to his extensive experience gained through various wanderings and journeys, as well as his great wisdom (which is constantly tested by the rest of the company's incessant questions). However, unlike Thorin, he displays great humility when his skills fail him: he does not hesitate to ask other characters such as Elrond, Beorn and even the eagles for help in completing his difficult quest.

As well as acting as a leader, he also plays the role of a helper, and gets the other characters out of any number of scrapes thanks to his quick thinking and his magic (for example, he is keeps the trolls confused until the sunlight turns them to stone, and invents a spell that allows the dwarves to escape from the goblins' cave). It therefore comes as no surprise that the company makes several unsuccessful attempts to prevent their guide from leaving them to attend to more pressing concerns. Gandalf does not return to continue helping the group until the end of the story, when he warns them about the approaching goblins and wolves.

SMAUG

Smaug is a cruel, greedy dragon, and is the main foe that Thorin and his company face during their quest. Like all dragons, he is obsessed with gold, and this, coupled with his own greed and cruelty, drove him to destroy the dwarf kingdom of the Lonely Mountain so that he could claim its immeasurable riches for himself. After this successful attack, he remains in the mountain to watch over his hoard. Because of his reluctance to leave the mountain, he does not actually make an appearance until quite late in the novel, and the reader is only told about him through secondhand stories prior to his conversation with Bilbo.

Aside from his fiery breath and his strength, the dragon's cunning is without a doubt the greatest danger the company faces: the dragon detects their presence in his lair almost immediately, but does not react in any way, hoping to escape their notice. When the hobbit comes to talk to him, protected by the ring's power, Smaug answers his questions in the hope of locating the intruder and killing him with his flames. He does not believe that any opponent could possibly outsmart him, and it is this excessive self-confidence that eventually leads him to his doom. His immense pride leads him to show off his gemstone armour to the hobbit, not realising that the hobbit has noticed its weak spot. The thrush then informs Bard of this weakness, which enables the archer to vanquish the monster once and for all.

GOLLUM

Bilbo meets Gollum after he escapes from the goblins. Gollum lives alone beside an underground lake, and has been shaped by these surroundings. He is described as short, old, dark and slimy. In addition to his repulsive appearance, he is a deceitful, cruel creature who clearly suffers from schizophrenia, and whose origins are shrouded in mystery.

As soon as he lays eyes on Bilbo, he instantly dreams of eating him. In order to do so, he suggests a game of riddles – if Bilbo wins, Gollum will show him the way out of the caves, but if Bilbo loses, he will become Gollum's next meal. And so begins the fool's game between the two characters, with Bilbo eventually proving himself cleverer than Gollum's trickery. Thanks to the magic ring that was Gollum's only possession, and which Bilbo unwittingly stole from him, the hobbit is able to evade his clutches, leaving Gollum alone in his despair. Losing the ring is an absolute tragedy in Gollum's eyes, as he has developed a real obsession with it. Realising that he has been tricked, he swears eternal hatred for Bilbo, which will eventually have very real consequences in *The Lord of the Rings*.

BARD

Bard is a descendant of the last ruler of one of the towns ravaged by Smaug. He is gradually introduced through the narrator and the inhabitants of Esgaroth. Although he is initially described as "grim-voiced and grim-faced" (p. 228), which might seem to indicate a somewhat disagreeable character, he is the only one who realises that the dragon is about to attack and organises a defence in the nick of time. He is also one of the few people who refuse to flee, and is the one who manages to slay the dragon thanks to the thrush, who tells him of Smaug's weak spot. Later on, he is the one who tries to hold peaceful negotiations with Thorin by acting as a spokesman for multiple factions (humans and elves).

His initially intimidating appearance, his noble lineage, his foresight, his courage and his ability to bring several factions together all seem to foreshadow the character of Aragorn in *The Lord of the Rings*.

ANALYSIS

ACTANTIAL MODEL

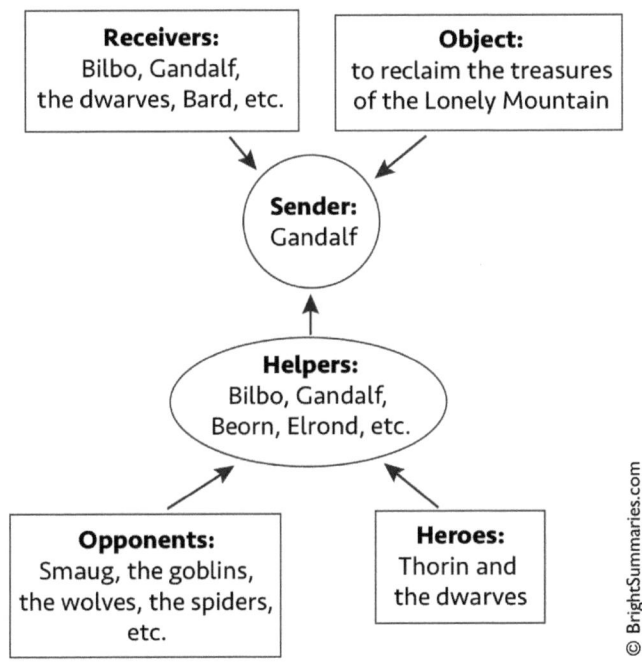

NARRATIVE OUTLINE

Initial situation: this is the start of the story, the time for setting the scene and introducing the characters; the situation is balanced, meaning that there is no reason for it to change.

- Bilbo Baggins is a hobbit who leads a peaceful, comfortable life in his hobbit-hole.

Disruptive element: this is an event that happens, changing the initial situation and triggering the real story.

- The wizard Gandalf whisks Bilbo off on adventure to act as the burglar for a company of 13 dwarves.

Developments: these are the events caused by the disruptive element which lead the hero to take action to solve the problem.

- First of all, the group is captured by trolls, and then by goblins, but they are saved by Gandalf each time. However, as they are fleeing the goblins' lair, Bilbo falls into a chasm where he finds Gollum's magic ring and wins the game of riddles. After being rescued by the eagles,

Thorin and his followers visit Beorn's house, then head to Mirkwood forest, where the wizard bids them farewell. The dwarves are attacked by giant spiders and then imprisoned by the wood-elves, and only escape thanks to Bilbo. They float down the river in barrels to reach Lake-town, then head to the Lonely Mountain, which they enter through a secret door. Bilbo is sent ahead as a scout, and steals a golden cup, then the Arkenstone, before having a conversation with Smaug. Realising that he has been tricked, the dragon retaliates by attacking the inhabitants of Lake-town, but Bard slays him. He demands compensation from Thorin, who refuses to pay up, so Bilbo hands the Arkenstone over to Bard in order to smooth things over. However, his efforts backfire, and Thorin exiles him for treason. When Dain's army arrives, it triggers a battle, which is brought to a standstill when Gandalf warns them that the goblins and wolves are marching towards them. Upon hearing this, the former enemies band together for the Battle of Five Armies, during which Thorin is killed.

Outcome: this puts an end to the developments and leads to the conclusion.

- Thorin is killed, but the battle is won and each character is rewarded.

Conclusion: this is the end of the story. The situation is stable again, like the initial situation, but it has undergone some changes.

- Bilbo finally returns home to his peaceful life.

A FAIRY TALE

The Hobbit is a story which was originally written for children. Given this target audience and the elements that Tolkien wanted to include in the story, the writing it as a tale was the natural choice. Tales are characterised by:

- imaginary and often fantastical happenings;
- their dual functions of entertaining and conveying a moral message;
- being handed down by oral tradition long before being put to paper.

Each of these characteristics is echoed in the plot of *The Hobbit*:

- The novel is saturated with fantastic elements ("fantastic" in this context meaning supernatural elements with no rational explanation), both in terms of beasts (goblins, fierce wolves, trolls, etc.) and the characters themselves (Gandalf's magic powers, Beorn's ability to transform into a bear, the terrifying Gollum or even the imaginary races like the dwarves and the elves), as well as objects (the way Sting glows blue in the presence of danger, the ring's powers of invisibility, the Arkenstone, etc.) and even the events themselves (the stone giants' attack, the anthropomorphic animals at Beorn's house).

- All of the characters' adventures are told in a light, humorous tone so as to create an enjoyable reading experience. For this reason, the author includes a great deal of comedy throughout the book by means of exaggeration (Gandalf's enormous breakfast at Beorn's house), teasing (the dwarves jokingly threaten to break Bilbo's dishes), or surprise (Bilbo is attacked by a giant spider while he is in the middle of thinking about his home). Although several scenes are suffused with both tension and humour, Tolkien also takes a more solemn tone when called for (for example during the Battle of Five Armies or Thorin's death), perhaps wanting to show that the violence of reality can easily lurk just below the surface of a deceptively innocent narrative. This approach further reinforces the moral of the story: that appearances can be deceiving. In fact, the reader's preconceived notions about Bilbo, Gandalf and Thorin are all turned on their heads over the course of the story.

- Finally, while it is likely that the story was told aloud a few times before being written down, its oral dimension is most in evidence within the text itself. This is due to the author's narrative style – in addition to making frequent interjections in the first person, he uses a style that makes it seem as though the story is being told aloud to an audience of young children. He also makes frequent comments about the characters' actions, explains what conclusions can be drawn from certain events, gives the characters certain characteristics which he then refers to repeatedly, and uses onomatopoeia on numerous occasions to mimic the noise of an object or event (for example, "splash" when Bilbo falls in the water, p. 67).

THE THEME OF JOURNEYS

Journeys are an omnipresent, twofold theme in *The Hobbit*. Of course, Tolkien, or at least the narrator, sweeps both Bilbo and the reader off on a journey in the traditional sense of the word. This journey is generally referred to within the story itself through long, specific descriptions of the places visited by the characters. Furthermore, each new chapter corresponds to a new stage in the characters' journey. Lastly, the most innovative aspect of the book also contributes to this theme: it includes maps which were hand-drawn by Tolkien himself, which allow the reader to follow the route the characters take on their quest.

But there is also a more symbolic, psychological journey. This is most obviously true of the eponymous hobbit – Bilbo is a homebody who has been thrown into an adventure he has no real stake in, who can frequently be heard complaining "I wish I was at home in my nice hole by the fire, with the kettle just beginning to sing!" (p. 30). This phrase, coupled with the narrator's commentary ("It was not the last time that he wished that!" p. 30), becomes a leitmotif that reappears frequently throughout the novel, and as such is a considerable source of comic relief. However, this character, who is almost entirely overshadowed by his travelling companions, gains confidence and stature after he commits his first burglary by stealing Gollum's ring. With the help of this precious item, he saves his travelling companions from danger on several occasions, and it is not long before they begin trusting him completely. However, he is not the only one who develops and grows psychologically and rises to the challenge of becoming a hero: Bard undergoes a similar journey. He is initially held in low esteem by the other inhabitants of Esgaroth, but he lives up to his heritage by organising the defence of the town when the dragon approaches, as well as slaying the beast. From then on, the rest of the town considers him a hero, even though they had never been fond of his pessimism: "'We will have King Bard!' the people near at hand shouted in reply" (p. 230). In the same way that Gandalf sings Bilbo's praises to the dwarves ("Mr. Baggins has more about him than you guess" p. 88), the old raven advises the dwarves to trust Bard: "trust […] him that shot the dragon with his bow. Bard is he, of the race of Dale, of the line of

Girion; he is a grim man but true" (p. 236).

MYTHOLOGICAL INFLUENCES

In *The Silmarillion*, *The Hobbit* and *The Lord of the Rings*, Tolkien created an entire wide-ranging universe with its own mythology and even its own languages. However, some references to other mythologies also appear in Tolkien's writing, particularly in *The Hobbit*. Some of these references are more veiled than others, and the most obvious ones tend to be drawn from Greco-Roman mythology, which is also the mythological tradition that readers would generally be most familiar with. For example, Gollum's role in the story is reminiscent of the Sphinx, a monster from Greek mythology which blocks the hero's path and refuses to let them pass unless they answer the creature's riddles correctly.

However, Gollum is not just a reimagining of the Sphinx. He also seems to share certain traits with Grendel, one of the monsters from *Beowulf* (700-1000 C.E.), an Anglo-Saxon legend which Tolkien was an expert on. Aside from sharing the same initial (like Bilbo and Beowulf), they both live in an unhealthy environment: Grendel lived in marshes, while Gollum lives beside an underground lake. The dragon, who guards an underground hoard of treasure, may also have been inspired by this epic poem, which features a dragon whose "pent-up fury at the loss of the vessel made him long to hit back and lash out in flames" (ll. 2304-2306). Furthermore, both heroes name their swords: Bilbo's is called "Sting", while Beowulf's is called "Hrunting". Finally, the narrator of the poem also has a strong presence and uses the personal pronoun "I" to express himself, the same way Tolkien does in his own story.

All of these elements combine to create a captivating story which immerses its reader in the story right from the beginning. *The Hobbit* has been very positively received, both in the United Kingdom and in the United States. Nowadays, what was once a simple children's tale has become a landmark of popular culture, and the novel was even adapted into a film trilogy by Peter Jackson in 2012.

FURTHER REFLECTION

SOME QUESTIONS TO THINK ABOUT...

- Take another look at the style the songs in the book are written in. How are they representative of each race (elves, dwarves, humans)?
- How does Tolkien portray time?
- In your opinion, what is the narrative purpose of personifying objects?
- Discuss and comment on this statement by the narrator: "Now it is a strange thing, but things that are good to have and days that are good to spend are soon told about, and not much to listen to; while things that are uncomfortable, palpitating, and even gruesome, may make a good tale, and take a deal of telling anyway" (p. 48).
- In what way is the novel a good illustration of the popular saying "Two hands are better than one"?
- List some of the comedic elements of the story.

- Do you know of any other books in which the narrator addresses the reader directly? What effect does this have on the reader?
- In your opinion, which elements of *The Hobbit* foreshadow *The Lord of the Rings*?
- Discuss and comment on this quote from C. S. Lewis, the author of *The Chronicles of Narnia*, who published an anonymous review saying, "*The Hobbit* [...] will be funnier to its youngest readers, and only years later, at a tenth or a twentieth reading, will they begin to realise what deft scholarship and profound reflection have gone to make everything in it so ripe, so friendly, and in its own way so true. Prediction is dangerous: but *The Hobbit* may well prove a classic."
- Fantasy is a popular genre among teenagers, as is science fiction. Why is this, in your opinion?

We want to hear from you!
Leave a comment on your online library
and share your favourite books on social media!

FURTHER READING

REFERENCE EDITION

- Tolkien, J. R. R. (2011) *The Hobbit*. London: HarperCollins.

REFERENCE STUDIES

- Drout, M. D. C. ed. (2006) *J.R.R. Tolkien Encyclopedia: Scholarship and Critical Assessment*. New York: Routledge.

- Tolkien, C. and Tolkien, J. R. R. (2014) *Beowulf: A Translation and Commentary*. London: HarperCollins.

ADAPTATIONS

- *The Hobbit: An Unexpected Journey*; *The Hobbit: The Desolation of Smaug*; *The Hobbit: The Battle of the Five Armies*. (2012-2014) [Film trilogy]. Peter Jackson. Dir. New Zealand/USA: WingNut Films, New Line Cinema, Metro-Goldwyn-Mayer, Warner Bros. Pictures.

- *The Hobbit*. (1977) [TV film]. Arthur Rankin, Jr. and Jules Bass. Dir. USA/Japan: ABC Video Enterprises,

Topcraft, Rankin/Bass, Warner Bros. Television Distribution.

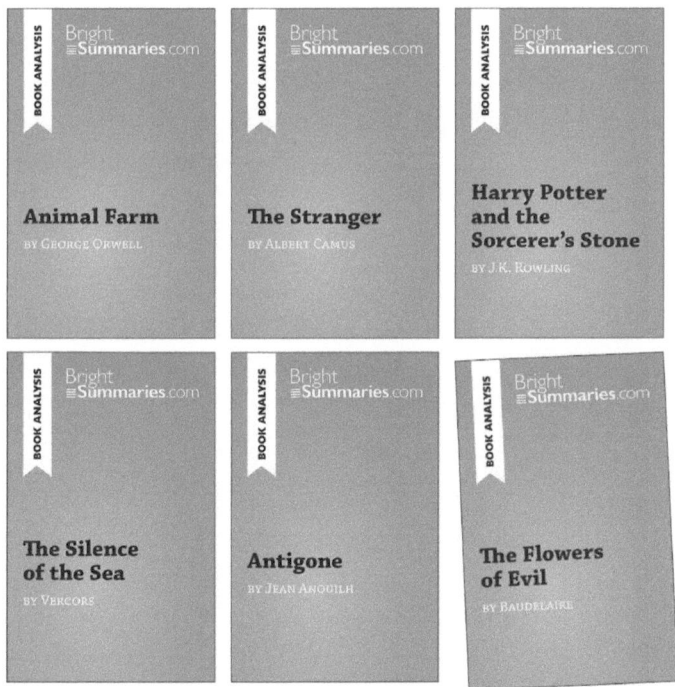

www.brightsummaries.com

Ebook EAN: 9782806296368

Paperback EAN: 9782806296375

Legal Deposit: D/2017/12603/210

Cover: © Primento

Digital conception by Primento, the digital partner of
publishers.